Contemporary African Americans
TONI MORRISON

BY
DIANE PATRICK-WEXLER

RSVP
RAINTREE
STECK-VAUGHN
P U B L I S H E R S
The Steck-Vaughn Company

Austin, Texas

Published by Raintree Steck-Vaughn, an imprint of Steck-Vaughn Company.
Produced by Mega-Books, Inc.
Design and Art Direction by Michaelis/Carpelis Design Associates.
Cover photo: ©Erin Elder/Saba

Library of Congress Cataloging-in-Publication Data
Patrick-Wexler, Diane.
  Toni Morrison/by Diane Patrick-Wexler.
      p.   cm. — (Contemporary African Americans)
  Includes bibliographical references (p. 47) and index.
  Summary: Discusses the personal life and literary achievements of the woman who, in 1993, became the first African American to win the Nobel Prize in Literature.
    ISBN 0-8172-3987-1 (Hardcover)
    ISBN 0-8172-6876-6 (Softcover)
    1. Morrison, Toni,—Juvenile literature.   2. Afro-American women novelists—20th century—Biography—Juvenile literature.   3. African Americans—Biography—Juvenile literature.
[1. Morrison, Toni   2. Authors, American.   3. Women—Biography.]   I. Title.   II. Series.
PS3563. 08749Z822   1997
813' .54—dc21   96-45136
[B]   CIP
                                                           AC
Printed and bound in the United States.

1 2 3 4 5 6 7 8 9 LB 00 99 98 97 96

Photo credits: ©Falour/Stills/Retna LTD.: p. 4; ©Ulf Andersen/The Gamma Liaison Network: pp. 7, 10; Courtesy of Alfred A. Knopf: pp. 9, 29, 30, 33, 35; Courtesy of the Harvard University Archives/Joe Wrinn/Harvard University News Office: p. 12; The Bettmann Archive: pp. 15, 16; ©Michael Newman/PotoEdit: p. 19; AP/Wide World Photos: pp. 20, 24, 36, 40, 43; Moorland-Spingarn Research Center, Howard University Archives, Howard University: p. 23; ©Gregory Pace/Retna LTD.: p. 27; ©Danny Hoffman/Sygma: p. 39; ©Chris Brown/Saba: p.44.

Contents

Chapter One

STORIES OF PAINFUL LIVES

On Thursday, October 7, 1993 author Toni Morrison awoke in her New Jersey home at 4:30 A.M. to write. At 7 A.M. the phone rang, startling her. "I knew it was terrible news," she has said.

But it was Ruth Simmons, a colleague from Princeton University. "Did you hear?" Ruth asked.

Toni thought something awful had happened.

"You have won the Nobel Prize for literature!"

The Nobel Prize in literature is one of the most important prizes a writer can win. Authors cannot apply for this award. Instead a list of nominees is drawn up by previous Nobel Prize winners, professors, and writers' organizations. This list is given to the Swedish Academy of Literature in Stockholm,

Toni Morrison was the first African-American woman to win the Nobel Prize.

Sweden. Then the Academy chooses a winner. It is given every year to an author, on the basis of all of his or her work, by the Swedish Academy of Literature. Winning this award was one of Toni Morrison's proudest moments.

Many people have only faint memories of their childhood. But Toni Morrison's memories of growing up have helped her to write prizewinning **novels.** Toni Morrison's stories paint a picture of the African-American community. She represents black culture in her writing, using fiction to show readers how African-American people live and act. These books have made her one of the most celebrated African-American authors of our time.

Her childhood experiences and memories involve the language, stories, music, myths, and rituals that she saw and heard around her. Her parents told ghost stories. Her mother sang. Her grandmother kept a book that explained the meaning of dreams. The people around her believed in magic and visits from spirits. Years later Toni would explain this mysterious world of black American culture through her novels.

As a child Toni became fascinated by the speech of ordinary black people. To her ears the language mixed Biblical passages, preaching, and street slang. She loved hearing it and includes it in her novels.

"She paints pictures with words," says opera star Leontyne Price, "and reading or hearing those words is like listening to music."

To portray African-American culture in her novels, Toni Morrison uses her own life experiences and those of her ancestors.

In Toni Morrison's stories, there is often a person who acts strangely but in a harmless or charming way. "There is always an elder there to guide them," Toni has said, "and these ancestors are not just parents, they are sort of timeless people . . . they provide a certain kind of wisdom."

Many people have tried to explain Toni Morrison's writing, using fancy language and long explanations. In fact it may be helpful to read about her books before actually reading them because it is important to know what her words mean. But a simple explanation is that Toni's stories are about how the black community affects the characters. Some critics describe her novels as negative portrayals of black life. But in all of her stories, staying true to the culture is more important than having a happy ending. Her books also carry the idea that the connection to one's ancestors is what keeps one truly alive and happy. Although they are easy to read, her novels are filled with complex characters and emotions. Toni's books must be read slowly, or several times, to understand their entire meaning.

Her characters often have unusual names, like Milkman Dead, Chicken Little, BoyBoy, Son, and First Corinthians. In her stories there are dreams, ghosts, and people who try to fly. Sometimes the events in the stories are not told in the order in which they happen. She frequently uses flashbacks. A flashback is when an author interrupts the story to tell about something that happened earlier. And sometimes these are unhappy events such as deaths and accidents.

Morrison's first two novels are about growing up young, female, and black in America. These were experiences of black women that no one had written about before. *The Bluest Eye*, published in 1969, tells the story of a young black girl whose desire for blue eyes drives her insane. *Sula*, published in 1973, is about the lifelong friendship between Sula, a woman who opposes the values of the community, and her friend Nel, a woman who supports the values. The community avoids Sula, but she is never actually driven away. *Sula* was nominated for a National Book Award in 1975, and it also won the Ohioana Book Award in 1975.

Song of Solomon, published in 1977, is about a young man named Milkman Dead. He searches for a family treasure in the caves of Virginia but ends up finding something even more valuable instead—the songs, myths, and stories of his ancestors. In this story Morrison shows the importance of connecting with the past.

In *Tar Baby* Jadine, a beautiful black model, finds herself torn between the rich, white world of Paris

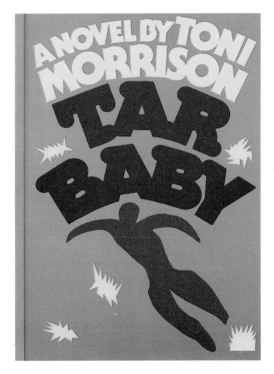

Tar Baby, a book about racial fears, was published in 1981 and was on the best-seller list for four months.

The oral tradition is an important aspect of African-American culture, whether it is storytelling or story reading. Here Toni Morrison reads to a group from her novel *Beloved*.

and the world of her black boyfriend. Again, the unavoidable connection with the past is an important theme. Published in 1981, *Tar Baby* was on the best-seller list for four months.

In *Beloved*, published in 1987, a runaway slave named Sethe kills her baby daughter so that the child will not have to grow up as a slave. Part of the story is told from the point of view of the slain daughter. *Beloved* won the Pulitzer Prize in 1988. The Pulitzer Prizes are a group of awards that have been presented yearly since 1917. The prizes are among the most important awards a writer can win. They are given for achievement by Americans in **literature**, drama, music, and journalism.

In *Jazz*, published in 1992, Morrison wrote about New York City in the 1920s. It is the story of Violet and Joe Trace, a married couple who live in Harlem in 1926. *Jazz* is the second in a trilogy, or series of three (that began with *Beloved*), about black life during important historical periods.

Toni Morrison has always lived in the world of words. An eager reader since childhood, she went on to earn college degrees in English and in English literature. These degrees qualified her to work as a professor of literature as well as a book **editor**. As a professor she taught and wrote critical essays. As an editor at Random House, a large **publishing company**, she helped to bring the works of other black writers to print. With her help works by such black authors as Muhammad Ali, Toni Cade Bambara, Angela Davis, and Gayl Jones were published.

By 1970 newspapers and magazines were asking her opinion about black life and black books. Between 1971 and 1972, she reviewed 28 books and wrote an important essay on the women's liberation movement for *The New York Times*.

In 1990 at Harvard University, she gave an important lecture series, called the "Massey Lectures in American Civilization." Her subject was blackness (or Africanism, as she calls it) in literature by white writers. The lectures were published in 1992 as *Playing in the*

Toni Morrison (bottom row, left) received an honorary degree from Harvard University in 1989.

Dark: Whiteness and the Literary Imagination.

Morrison was commissioned, or asked, to write a play in honor of the first national observance of Dr. Martin Luther King, Jr.'s birthday. The play, *Dreaming Emmett*, was based on the life of young Emmett Till, a black boy who was killed by racist whites in Mississippi in 1954. The play was performed by an Albany, New York theater company in 1986. She was also commissioned by Carnegie Hall to write lyrics for *Honey and Rue*, an opera performed there in 1992, starring black soprano Kathleen Battle.

In May 1992 Toni Morrison became the first author to have books on both the fiction and nonfiction *New*

York Times best-seller lists. *Jazz* was on the fiction list at number five, and *Playing in the Dark: Whiteness and the Literary Imagination* was number 16 on the nonfiction list.

Toni Morrison has received honorary degrees from many American colleges and universities, including Columbia University, Dartmouth College, Harvard University, Spelman College, and Yale University.

Now, twice a week at Princeton University in New Jersey, Toni Morrison teaches "Studies in American Africanism" to a class of 12 students. The course discusses how Africans and their descendants are reflected in American literature.

STORYTELLING EVERY DAY

On February 18, 1931 Toni Morrison was born Chloe Anthony Wofford in Lorain, Ohio. Lorain is near the shores of Lake Erie, one of the five Great Lakes. Lorain is also close to the Ohio River, which was important in moving people on the **Underground Railroad**. The railroad was not a real railroad, but a network or group of people who helped thousands of slaves to escape to freedom in the North or in Canada. The slaves traveled only by night and were in constant fear that they would be caught and sold, or even killed. Because Lorain was near the Underground Railroad, it had a large black community.

Chloe Anthony Wofford was the second of four children of George and Ramah Wofford. Her maternal grandparents, Ardelia and John Solomon Willis, had been sharecroppers in Greenville, Alabama. In the late 1890s, her grandfather was cheated out of

Lorain, Ohio, Toni Morrison's birthplace, was a stopping place on the Underground Railroad.

the 88 acres of his Native American mother's land by cruel whites. After that the family was never able to get out of debt. This and other such experiences convinced John Solomon that there was no hope for black people in America. His wife, Ardelia, disagreed and preferred to place her trust in God. To earn money, John Solomon, who played violin, went to Birmingham, Alabama, to work as a musician and sent his earnings home to Ardelia.

"But my grandmother began to get nervous, all alone in Greenville," Morrison has said, "because her daughters were reaching puberty, which was a dangerous business in the South, in the country, where white boys began to notice the girls."

So Ardelia decided to leave. She sent her husband a message: "We're heading north on the midnight train. If you ever want to see us again, you'll be on that train."

When the family met up again, they traveled to Kentucky, where John Solomon worked in a coal mine, and Ardelia did other people's laundry. The children went to a little one-room schoolhouse.

"One day," Morrison recounts, "the teacher, who was about 16 and white, was doing long division and

Toni Morrison's mother attended a one-room school much like this one, the oldest schoolhouse in the country, located in St. Augustine, Florida.

[was] having trouble explaining it. Since my mother and her sister already knew long division, they explained it to the teacher and to the class.

"They came home all excited and proud of themselves, crowing, 'Mama, guess what we did? We taught the teacher long division!' My grandmother turned to her husband and said, 'Come on, Johnny, we have to move.'" She knew that white people at that time did not take kindly to black children who were smarter than their teachers.

They continued north, finally settling in Lorain. Their daughter Ramah, Chloe's mother, grew up to be a feisty, determined woman. She was open-minded and patient when dealing with white people and was an expert at handling thoughtless landlords and social workers. "When an eviction notice was put on our house, she tore it off," Morrison remembers. "If there were maggots in our flour, she wrote a letter to President Franklin Roosevelt."

George Wofford, Chloe Anthony's father, was a hardworking man. Yet like her grandfather, he'd had terrible experiences with white people. Therefore, he distrusted "every word and every gesture of every white man on Earth."

As Chloe Anthony grew older, she heard family stories about something that had happened when she was two years old. Once, when her parents were unable to pay the monthly rent of four dollars, the angry landlord tried to burn down the house with the family still inside! That story about hatred was one Chloe Anthony would remember all her life and later include in her writing.

"My father was a racist," Morrison has said. "As a child in Georgia, he received shocking impressions of adult white people, and for the rest of his life he felt he was justified in despising all whites, and that they were not justified in despising him." He did his best to keep white people out of his life.

However, his racist attitudes did not rub off on his children. "I knew he was wrong," Morrison remembers. "I went to school with white children—they were my friends. There was no awe, no fear . . . . When I was in first grade, nobody thought I was inferior. I was the only black [child] in the class and the only child who could read!"

Her parents' differing attitudes toward whites had an effect on the way Chloe Anthony saw the lives of blacks. Both parents agreed that all the love and help they needed came from their family and their community. Little Chloe Anthony could see this every day. Everything everyone did, both in the family and in the neighborhood, made a difference in someone else's life.

Everyone in the community cared about the local children. If they misbehaved they would be scolded by whichever adult was nearby. Then their parents would be told! Of course the children, including Chloe Anthony, hated it.

Storytelling was an important part of Toni Morrison's childhood. Storytellers like the one pictured here help preserve black culture.

"That was also something that made me feel, 'Oh, boy, wait till I get out of this place, because I am tired of all these people who can meddle with me,'" she remembers. Although now she admits that she appreciates the care and concern that the adults of her community had for all the children.

When Chloe Anthony was young, storytelling was the main form of family entertainment. All the grown-ups in the family participated. This is how Chloe Anthony learned the cultural rituals of her family and community. Her mother sang in the church choir; her grandfather played the violin; and her grandmother used a "dream book." This was a book that explained the meaning of dreams. And many other people often told of visits from ghosts and spirits. These family and community gatherings formed Chloe Anthony's strongest childhood memories.

But reading was the most exciting part of little Chloe Anthony's life. Before she entered first grade, her parents had taught her to read at home. The family often spent some of its hard-earned money on books. Chloe Anthony's mother belonged to a book club, and when new books arrived, the little girl felt a great pleasure and security.

Chloe Anthony read everything. As a teenager she read English translations of classic French and Russian

Receiving the Nobel Prize in literature on December 16, 1993 was the crowning achievement of Toni Morrison's lifelong love of reading and literature.

novels. She was fascinated by the way the writers presented their cultures in their writing. She felt as if the writing spoke to everyone—even those who were not a part of those cultures. "Those books were not written for a little black girl in Lorain, Ohio," she has said, "but they were so magnificently done that I understood them anyway."

When Chloe Anthony was 12, she had to get a job to help with the family expenses. At age 13 she cleaned house for a white family after school. One day she complained to her father because the work was hard, and the woman was mean. He said, "Girl, you don't live there. You live *here*. So you go do your work, get your money, and come on home."

"I remember a very important lesson that my father gave me when I was 12 or 13. He said, 'You know, today I welded a perfect seam, and I signed my name to it.' And I said, 'But Daddy, no one's going to see it!' And he said, 'Yeah, but I know it's there.' So when I was working in kitchens, I did good work."

Even though the family was very poor, their parents made the children feel as if they were very important. "Growing up in Lorain, my parents made all of us feel as though there were these rather extraordinary, deserving people within us," Morrison remembers. "I felt like an aristocrat—or what I think an aristocrat is. I always knew we were very poor. But that was never degrading."

Three

A WORLD
OF WORDS

In 1949 Chloe Anthony graduated with honors from Lorain High School. After high school Chloe Anthony's family expected her to find a job, get married, and settle down. She thought about becoming a dancer—but not for long. "It's not as though I were a little perfect dancer with a little blond topknot," she has often said. "What I did extremely well was read."

So Chloe Anthony went to Howard University, an all-black school, to study for a degree in English. She picked Howard because she thought it would be full of smart black students who would stimulate her mind. "But that was not what the school was about," she has said. "It was about getting married, buying clothes, and going to parties."

To be around students who were interested in hard work, Chloe Anthony, who had shortened her name to Toni, joined the Howard University Players, a

Toni Morrison performed with the Howard University Players in *Richard III*.

campus theater group. She traveled with the group during the summers, performing in plays in the South. This was her first time traveling through the South, and she was finally able to see the life that the grown-ups in her family had told her about.

In 1953 Toni graduated with a bachelor's degree in English. She decided to go to Cornell University for a graduate degree in English, mainly because, as she put it, she had "nowhere to go." She spent long hours studying in the library, and in 1955 she received a master's degree in English.

Toni's degrees qualified her to teach. For the next two years, she taught English at Texas Southern

Four years after she had graduated from Howard University, Toni Morrison returned there to teach. Among her students was civil rights activist Stokely Carmichael.

University in Houston, Texas. Then, in 1957 she accepted an appointment to teach English at her old school, Howard University. She held this position until 1964. Some of her students became famous: Claude Brown, author of *Manchild in the Promised Land* and *Children of Ham*; and Stokely Carmichael, a civil rights activist in the 1960s, later known as Kwame Ture.

While teaching at Howard University, Toni met Harold Morrison, a Washington architecture student of Jamaican ancestry. They married in 1958. But the marriage, which Toni refuses to discuss, was difficult. To ease her unhappiness, she began to write stories. "It was as though I had nothing left but my imagination," she recalls. "I had no will, no judgment, no perspective, no power, no authority, no self—just . . . a trembling respect for words. I wrote like someone with a dirty habit. Secretly. Compulsively. Slyly."

Soon Toni joined a group of ten black poets and writers in Washington, D.C. They met once a month to read, discuss, and criticize one another's work. For awhile Toni brought stories she had written in high school. One day, having nothing from the old collection to take to the meeting, she quickly wrote a story about a young black girl who wanted blue eyes. The idea came from a conversation Toni had had as a child with another black girl. The girl had refused to believe in God when her prayers for blue eyes had not been answered after two years.

In 1964 Toni's marriage ended, leaving her a divorced mother of two young sons, Harold Ford and Slade Kevin. Because of demands by civil rights groups during this time, many publishing companies were revising their textbooks. In 1965 Toni was offered a job as textbook editor at L.B. Singer, a division of Random House Publishing. The company was located in Syracuse, New York. Toni accepted the job and moved to Syracuse with her sons.

Because Toni's job took a lot of time, and because she was new to Syracuse, she had few friends. So while coworkers were going to parties or dinners, Toni stayed home and wrote. She started building on the story about the little black girl who wanted blue eyes. What are the effects, she wondered, on a black girl who longs to look like a white girl?

In 1968 she was transferred to the company's New York City office. She became senior editor and stayed with the company until 1983. At the time she was the only black woman to hold such a position, and she became a well-respected editor. Toni used her influence to help publish the works of black writers.

Being an editor and a single parent were not the only things that Toni did at that time. More than anything Toni loved to help young people discover their creative talents. So she continued to teach black literature and creative writing.

As she edited the manuscripts of other writers, she often wondered: Where were the stories about black girls and women like herself or the ones she knew? Where were the stories about people like her relatives in Lorain?

After awhile Toni got tired of books about black life that only talked about the leaders. She came up with an idea to create a black history book that showed how ordinary black people lived. The title would be *The Black Book*. Although her name does not appear in it, Toni was the book's editor at Random House.

The Black Book is a record of black life from slavery to the 1940s. It is filled with items that were found in attics, scrapbooks, and trunks. Toni hired four collectors who helped her gather material for the book. *The*

As a writer, editor, and critic, Toni Morrison is well respected by the publishing industry as well as by the reading public.

Black Book contains folktales, songs, jokes, newspaper clippings, and sheet music; announcements of weddings, births, and deaths; and photographs and letters.

As Toni worked on the project, she made many fascinating discoveries. There was a magazine article about a slave woman who had killed her children rather than have them returned to slavery with her. Toni also discovered the **patents** of inventions by African Americans, along with photographs of Harlem life. Harlem is a New York City neighborhood that is a center of black life and culture. Toni didn't realize it at the time, but the seeds of more stories were being planted in her mind.

THE BLUEST EYE AND BEYOND

Finally Toni's story about the little black girl who wished for blue eyes was finished. *The Bluest Eye* was published in 1969, by the Alfred A. Knopf publishing company, in New York City.

"I was really writing a book I wanted to read," she said. "I hadn't seen a book in which black girls were center stage."

The story is told by Claudia McTeer, a nine-year-old girl who lives in the Midwest, just as Toni did. It is the story of Claudia, her ten-year-old sister, Frieda, and their friend Pecola Breedlove. Pecola yearns to be like Shirley Temple, whom everyone in the black community adores. Feeling unloved by her family and the black community, Pecola equates being ugly with being black and decides that she is ugly. She becomes obsessed with the need to have blue eyes, which to her mean beauty. Her obsession drives her to madness.

Pecola's black friends, Claudia and Frieda, don't

worry about beauty and blue eyes. By telling Pecola's story, Claudia strives to understand why she and Frieda survived and Pecola did not. Because *The Bluest Eye* gave ordinary black girls a voice, it called attention to things about the lives of black American women that had never before been discussed.

There was only one problem with the publication of the book: On the cover, the author's name read "Toni Morrison," not "Chloe Anthony Morrison." When Toni saw the cover, she was very upset.

"They had the wrong name: Toni Morrison!" she lamented. "My name is Chloe Wofford. Toni's a nickname! I sort of knew it was going to happen. I

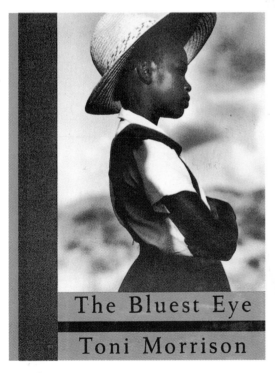

With *The Bluest Eye*, Toni Morrison was writing a story that she wanted to read when she was a girl.

was in a daze. I sent it in that way because the editor knew me as Toni Morrison. I write all the time about being misnamed. How you got your name is very special. My mother, my sister, all my family call me Chloe." But it was too late to change her name on the cover.

By this time, because of her work as a professor and an editor, Toni's opinions on black life and black books were widely sought. Her essays, articles, and book reviews in well-known newspapers and magazines gained Toni national recognition.

Still working as an editor in the daytime and writing at night, Toni completed *Sula*, her second novel, in 1973. Set in the 1940s, this novel examines

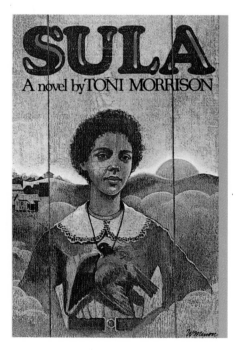

Sula, published in 1973, examines the friendship between two women. It earned Toni Morrison a National Book Award nomination.

a midwestern black community, called The Bottom. In *Sula* Morrison paints a picture of black girls after childhood and examines the importance of friendships between black women.

The story follows the lifelong friendship between Sula and Nel. The main character, Sula, does not care what the black community thinks of her, saying, "I know what every black woman in the country is doing. . . . Dying. Just like me. But the difference is they dying like a stump. Me, I'm going down like one of those redwoods." To prove her point, Sula does certain things that upset the black community: She puts her grandmother in a nursing home, and she begins dating white men. *Sula* was nominated for a National Book Award in 1975 and also won the Ohioana Book Award that same year.

Song of Solomon was Toni's next book, published in 1977. It came from her curiosity about how a person who left the black community to get an education could survive without self-destructive needs for material things. It is the story of Milkman Dead, a young man who tries to find a family fortune in the caves of Virginia. Although there is no fortune, he still finds something more important—an understanding of the history of his ancestors. *Song of Solomon* sold over three million copies and was on *The New York Times* best-seller list for 16 weeks.

After the financial success of *Song of Solomon*, Toni bought a house on the Hudson River. The day she first saw it, she walked along the dock and looked toward the river. She felt the voice of her father, who had died by then, expressing happiness with the place.

Song of Solomon was the first novel by a black writer to become a Book-of-the-Month Club selection since Richard Wright's novel *Native Son* was published in 1940. The novel's success earned awards, too. Toni received the National Book Critics Circle Award and was appointed to the American Academy and Institute of Arts and Letters. A year after its publication, when *Song of Solomon* was a paperback best-seller, President Jimmy Carter appointed Toni Morrison to the National Council of the Arts.

Her next book, 1981's *Tar Baby*, is set on a beautiful Caribbean island. The novel tells about the love affair between Jadine, a light-skinned black model who was educated in Europe, and Son, a dark-skinned escaped convict who hates white culture. Through their story Morrison discusses the racial fears sometimes felt by both whites and blacks. The book appeared on *The New York Times* best-seller list less than a month after it was published and remained there for four months.

Toni was becoming nationally famous. She made a long series of promotional tours and was on the cover of *Newsweek* magazine. And finally Morrison could afford to quit her day job. She resigned from Random House in 1983 to "do like the grown-ups do—live and write, and only do that."

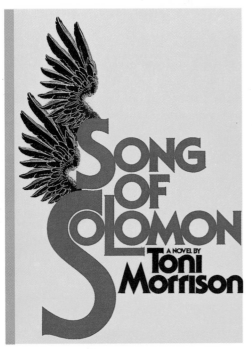

Song of Solomon is about a young man discovering the richness of his ancestry. The book became a national best-seller when it was published in 1977.

Yet Toni kept teaching. She was a Distinguished Visiting Professor at Yale University from 1975 to 1977. In 1984 she became Schweitzer Professor of the Humanities at the State University of New York at Albany. In 1989 she was appointed to the Robert F. Goheen Professorship in the Humanities Council at Princeton University in New Jersey. Toni taught creative writing, Afro-American studies, American studies, and women's studies. She moved to Princeton but kept the Hudson River house as a retreat.

Chapter

AN IMPORTANT PRIZE

When Toni Morrison began thinking about her next book, she remembered the magazine article about the slave woman who murdered her children. The woman believed death was better than slavery. That article was the inspiration for Toni's next novel, *Beloved*.

Here is what Toni has said about the story: "I imagined what would happen if this child could come back and say, 'How do you know death is better for me, since you've never done it?' That's where it started."

Set in Cincinnati, Ohio, a few years after slavery had ended, *Beloved* explores how Sethe, the mother who murdered her two-year-old daughter 18 years before, is haunted by the child's spirit. After the baby's ghost is driven from Sethe's home, a 20-year-old woman mysteriously appears in the town. She talks like a child and befriends Sethe, who believes the woman is the murdered infant returned to Earth. Sethe finally faces her guilt and seeks forgiveness from her daughter.

In January 1988, 50 black writers and critics wrote an open letter to *The New York Times Book Review* complaining that Toni Morrison had not yet won a National Book Award or Pulitzer Prize for her work. Among the signers were the poets Maya Angelou and Amiri Baraka, the novelists John Edgar Wideman and John A. Williams, and the critic Henry Louis Gates, Jr.

Toni said she did not know about the letter until its publication. "The furor that followed the publishing of that letter showed that it was an important thing to do," she said. "What that letter said was, 'your work is important to us.' This was from a range of writers across all political, gender, and age lines. It was interesting and unique. It made me feel blessed."

In April *Beloved* won the Pulitzer Prize. In accepting it, Toni remarked, "I'm very pleased to win it. Authors regard it as a singularly high achievement."

Beloved has been a widely read and studied book. It is taught in history, literature, creative writing, and women's studies courses. Toni decided that *Beloved* would be the first of three novels about black life from the 1800s to the present. The second novel, published in 1992, was called *Jazz*. The inspiration

Toni Morrison won the Pulitzer Prize in 1988 for *Beloved*.

came from a well-known photo of a young girl lying in a coffin by the famous Harlem Renaissance photographer James VanderZee.

Jazz tells the story of Joe Trace and his wife Violet, middle-aged sharecroppers (like Toni's grandparents) who moved to Harlem in 1926. Joe falls in love with Dorcas, an 18-year-old girl, but kills her when she tries to leave him. At the funeral, Violet slashes Dorcas's face in a fit of rage. Obsessed with learning everything she can about Dorcas, she confronts the girl's aunt. Eventually the two build a relationship where they respect each other even before they come to understand each other.

To celebrate the publication of *Jazz*, Toni's publisher, Knopf, threw a party at the elegant Four Seasons Restaurant in New York City. The city's first black mayor, David Dinkins, also attended the party with his wife. The evening's live entertainment featured a band with famous jazz musicians: saxophonist Frank Wess, trumpeter Doc Cheatham, bassist Milt Hinton, pianist Sir Roland Hanna, and drummer Al Halewood. It was truly a shining evening for one of literature's greatest women.

SHARING THE GIFTS

It took a long time for Toni to believe that she had won the Nobel Prize. On October 7, 1993, a few hours after her friend had called to tell her that she had won the prize, the secretary of the Swedish Academy called her to confirm the news. The prize carried a cash award of $825,000 and would be presented in December at a ceremony in Stockholm, Sweden. Toni Morrison was 62. She was the eighth woman and the first black woman to ever receive the prize.

"I said 'Why don't you send me a fax?'" Toni has said, recalling the moment. "Somehow, I felt that if I saw a fax, I'd know it wasn't a dream."

The official announcement was made that day by the Nobel Committee of the Swedish Academy. It stated, "Toni Morrison gives life to an essential aspect of American reality [in novels] characterized by visionary force and poetic import. She **delves** into the language itself, a language she wants to liberate from

Toni Morrison was a professor at Princeton University when she won the Nobel Prize in literature.

the **fetters** of race. And she addresses us with the luster of poetry."

Her publisher invited her to hold a press conference in New York, but she said no. She had to go to work. When she arrived at her Princeton University office, it was filled with flowers. Many people had faxed congratulations to her. There were television cameras and reporters all over the place. But she was a professor and had students to teach.

"The media outside were all wondering why she was going to class and whether she was still going to teach," said one of her students. "She laughed and thought that it was ridiculous that they would even ask."

When she finally did speak to reporters, she said, "This is a delight for me. It was wholly unexpected and so satisfying. Regardless of what we all say and truly believe about [the meaninglessness of] prizes and their relationship to the real work, nevertheless this is a signal honor for me.

"But what is most wonderful for me personally is to know that the Prize at last has been awarded to an African American. I thank God that my mother is alive to see this day."

Although she was already a best-selling author, the Nobel Prize made her books even more popular. Bookstores across the country quickly set up special tables and window displays of Toni Morrison's books

Swedish King Carl Gustaf XVI presents Toni Morrison with the Nobel Prize in literature at a ceremony in Stockholm, Sweden.

and had to order more copies of them because they were selling out. To honor her further, the Swedish Postal Service issued a stamp bearing a photo of her from 1977.

On December 7 she accepted the Nobel Prize as Chloe Anthony Wofford. Dressed in a long, sequined black gown, raspberry satin stole, and high heels, she gave a half-hour acceptance speech in Stockholm's Old City. She spoke calmly, as if reciting poetry to the crowd of more than 400 people. She spoke of the value of language.

It is words, she suggested, that fend off "the scariness of things with no names," and that "ease the burden of oppression."

The crowd gave her a standing ovation.

Later, at a party given by her publisher, she told friends that her entrance at the award ceremony was one of the most terrifying moments of her life. She thought that she would trip and fall while going down the long, marble staircase on the arm of the king of Sweden. "I'm not talking about six stairs," she said. "There must have been 90." She had looked down at the stairs and whispered to the king that she thought she was going to fall—and take him down with her!

"The king was very reassuring," she said. "He told me, 'We'll take care of each other. You hold on to me, and I'll hold on to you.'"

Henry Louis Gates, Jr., the chairman of the Afro-American Studies department at Harvard University, and the coeditor of a collection of essays on Toni Morrison's work, said, "Just two centuries ago, the African-American literary tradition was born in slave narratives. Now our greatest writer has won the Nobel Prize."

But a few short weeks later, on Christmas Day, fire destroyed Morrison's Hudson River home. It seems the fire was apparently started shortly after 9 A.M. by an ember that leaped from a fireplace onto a sofa. Her son Slade Kevin was alone in the house at the time.

"The ember landed on the couch, and he tried to put it out himself," said a police officer. "It got beyond his control. He called the fire department. They arrived within three or four minutes, and the flames were visible through the windows." It took five hours and some 100 firefighters to put out the flames. Slade escaped unhurt, but several firefighters received minor injuries. Toni was in Princeton at the time. Slade called her, and she rushed to the house, where she watched the last of the fire-fighting efforts.

"My manuscripts!" she cried. She was so desperate to retrieve the documents that she had to be talked out of going inside the burning building. She had promised to donate the manuscripts to the Schomburg Center for Research in Black Culture, a famous Harlem library. Fortunately the manuscripts were in a basement file cabinet and were not harmed.

Later Toni said, "I put the Nobel money away for my retirement. And then, of course, the minute I did

Toni's house was badly damaged in a fire in 1993. Fortunately her son, the only one at home at the time, escaped unharmed.

that, my house burned down. So, suddenly, I needed it and couldn't put my hands on it. It's probably just as well. Because if I hadn't done that, I would have taken the money and rebuilt my house, and it would have been like most of the money I've ever had—as soon as you get it, there's this big hole waiting for it.

"In the two years around the Nobel, I had a lot of bad luck, a lot of very serious devastations. My mother died, among other things. The only thing that happened that was unexpected and truly wonderful was the Nobel Prize. So I regard the fact that my house burned down after I won the Nobel Prize to be better than having my house burn down without

Toni Morrison is philosophical about the good and the bad things that have happened in her life and looks to the future with hope.

having won the Nobel Prize. Most people's houses just burn down. Period."

So what lies ahead for Toni Morrison? Her next project will be an anthology about the "social, racial, and political consequences" of the controversial O.J. Simpson case. The collection of essays is due to be published in the fall of 1996 and will be titled *Birth of a Nation-Hood: Gaze, Script and Spectacle in the O.J. Simpson Trial.*

In March 1994 Toni earned an honorary doctorate from the college she attended, Howard University. In the meantime Toni Morrison continues to observe black life and weave her observations into fascinating, best-selling stories.

1931   Born Chloe Anthony Wofford, on February 18, in Lorain, Ohio.

1949   Graduates with honors from Lorain High School.

1953   Graduates from Howard University; enrolls at Cornell University.

1955   Earns master's degree in English from Cornell University. Teaches English at Texas Southern University.

1957   Begins teaching English at Howard University.

1958   Marries Harold Morrison.

1964   Divorces Harold Morrison.

1969   First book, *The Bluest Eye*, is published.

1973   *Sula* is published.

1975   *Sula* is nominated for a National Book Award.

1977–1978   *Song of Solomon* is published. Wins National Book Critics Circle Award and American Academy and Institute of Arts and Letters Award.

1987   *Beloved* is published.

1988   Wins Pulitzer Prize for her novel *Beloved*.

1992   *Jazz* is published.

1993   Wins the Nobel Prize in literature.

delve   To investigate and look into.

editor   A person in a publishing house who recommends which new books should be published and helps authors to improve their writing.

fetters   Chains or ties that restrict the body or the mind.

literature   Writings that express ideas of permanent interest.

novel   A long, fictional story.

patent   An official document that says an inventor is the only one allowed to make, use, or sell an invention.

publishing company   A company that prepares and sells books.

Underground Railroad   A path used by slaves to escape to freedom before and during the Civil War.

Bibliography

Bell, Roseanne P. and others, editors. *Sturdy Black Bridges: Visions of Black Women in Literature*. Doubleday, 1979

Christian, Barbara. *Black Women Novelists: The Development of a Tradition, 1892–1976*. Greenwood Press, 1980.

Davis, Curt. "Toni Morrison and Her Wild Sula." *People*, March 18, 1974.

Index